12
STEP
WORKBOOK
FOR
EX-OFFENDERS

ISBN-10: 1461051886
EAN-13: 9781461051886
LCCN: 2011905328
Createspace, North Charleston, Sc

12
STEP
WORKBOOK
FOR
EX-OFFENDERS

∽〰〰〰〰〜

Brian Monroe CADC

Forward

On March 14, 2005 I was arrested and charged with my 13th Class X Drug felony. Over the preceding year, while on parole, I had been smoking in excess of an ounce of pure crack cocaine daily. I know it was pure crack because I was the one cooking it. Three days later, as the cocaine fog was leaving my brain, I heard a couple of voices. (No, I'm not a schizophrenic!) One was God requiring that I change the direction of my life and start serving Him by founding a ministry for ex-offenders. The second voice was that of the first servant God sent to me to assist with this ministry, Mr. Brian Monroe.

As I lay on my bunk in cell 1, 4 north pod and the drug induced fog was lifting from my brain I listened to Brian teaching the necessity of accountability. Slogans like "It starts with me and it ends with me", "putting myself into position" and "what part did I play in this" were absorbed into my empty brain like a dry sponge absorbs water.

F.I.S.T. Inc. was founded as a result of the early interaction between Brian Monroe and me. Our philosophy is one of service. AA and NA base their recovery on service work and we are no different. By providing service to the community our members have bonded with the community. They have been given opportunities that were not available to them before. As ex-offenders we must recognize that we have made mistakes and we must be willing to make amends not only to our victims, but to society as a whole. As Christians it is our responsibility to care for the least of us. If we support one another, "strive together" we can and will regain our rightful place in society. If we repent and ask His forgiveness we will retain our place in Heaven.

This guidebook is intended to be just that...a guidebook. To remain drug and crime free we -must apply the principles of the 12-step program and work it on a daily basis. If you need assistance, or someone to talk to, call the F.I.S.T. RESOURCE CENTER at 1-877-820-4571.

I want to thank Brian Monroe for taking on this daunting challenge, but acknowledge that his thoughts were guided by our Lord and Savior, Jesus Christ. Remember that you are not alone in your struggles. Our Lord and Savior will put people in your life to guide you, if you let Him.

God Bless You,

Joe Schmitt
President and Founder
F.I.S.T. Inc.
213 W. Water St.
Waukegan, IL 60085

Introduction

I know that we can change if we choose to and are motivated. I won't lie to you, the road at first, is tough but that can be the fun part of recovery; being determined that no matter what the hurdles are you can be strong enough to overcome them.

It is very difficult for many ex-offenders to accept that they must sometimes be dependent upon other people to assist them in changing their negative lifestyle. In the process of recovery you must become willing to trust someone to show you and lead you. In this workbook you will discover the thoughts, feelings and behaviors you currently practice and assist you through the process of changing them. This process of self change will assist you in the elimination of thoughts, feelings and behaviors that have been destroying your life, and based upon your motivation and desire to change, keep you criminal justice and prison free.

They have shown, and here are demonstrated for you, how people can with certainty "come to believe" what God can and will do to cure ex-offenders.

The **12 Steps** of Ex-Offenders Anonymous

Step 1   I admit I am powerless over my addiction to crime and/or drugs and alcohol and that my life has become unmanageable.

Step 2   I believe that a power greater than myself can restore me to sanity.

Step 3   I now make a conscious decision to turn my will and my life over to the care of God.

Step 4   I agree to a searching and fearless moral inventory of myself.

Step 5   I admit to God, to myself, and to at least one other human- being, the exact nature of my wrongs.

Step 6   I am entirely ready to have God remove all these defects of my character.

Step 7   I humbly asked God to remove my defects and shortcomings.

Step 8   I agree to make a list of all persons I have harmed and am willing to make amends to them all.

Step 9   I will make amends directly to such people wherever possible except when to do so would injure them or others.

Step 10   I will continue to take personal inventory and when I am wrong I will promptly admit it.

Step 11   I seek, through prayer and meditation, to improve my conscious contact with God, praying only for the knowledge of God's will for me and the power to carry that out.

Step 12   I, having had a spiritual awakening and as a result of an effort to practice these principles in my daily life, will carry this message to other ex offenders who have a desire to change.

THE TWELVE STEPS OF ALCOHOLICS ANONYMOUS

1. We admitted we were powerless over alcohol—that our lives had become unmanageable.

2. Came to believe that a Power greater than ourselves could restore us to sanity.

3. Made a decision to turn our will and our lives over to the care of God *as we understood Him.*

4. Made a searching and fearless moral inventory of ourselves.

5. Admitted to God, to ourselves, and to another human being the exact nature of our wrongs.

6. Were entirely ready to have God remove all these defects of character.

7. Humbly asked Him to remove our shortcomings.

8. Made a list of all persons we had harmed, and became willing to make amends to them all.

9. Made direct amends to such people wherever possible, except when to do so would injure them or others.

10. Continued to take personal inventory and when we were wrong promptly admitted it.

11. Sought through prayer and meditation to improve our conscious contact with God, *as we understood Him*, praying only for knowledge of His will for us and the power to carry that out.

12. Having had a spiritual awakening as the result of these Steps, we tried to carry this message to alcoholics, and to practice these principles in all our affairs.

12
STEP
WORKBOOK
FOR
EX-OFFENDERS

෴

Author: Brian Monroe, CADC
Edited by: Michael Bende
Illustrated by: Linda Samorez

Step 1

"I admit I am powerless over my addiction to crime and/or drugs and alcohol and that my life has become unmanageable."

1. Do you have a problem?

_____

_____

_____

2. Do you want to do something about it?

_____

_____

_____

3. What are you willing to do about it?

_____

_____

_____

4. Have you tried to stop your addiction to crime and/ drugs and alcohol?

_____

_____

_____

"For I will not trust in my bow,
neither shall my sword save me."
Psalm 44:6 (KJV)

"My disgrace is before me all day long,
and face is covered with shame."
Psalm 44:15 (NIV)

Step 2

"I believe that a power greater than myself can restore me to sanity."

"God is our refuge and strength, always ready to help in times trouble."
Psalm 46:1 (NLT)

"Now faith is the assurance of things hoped for, the conviction of things not seen. And without faith it is impossible to please Him, for he who comes to God must believe that He is and that He is a rewarder of those who seek Him. For nothing will be impossible with God."

1. What is my understanding of a Power Greater than myself today?

_____

_____

_____

2. Do I now believe, or am I even willing to believe that there is a Power greater than myself?

_____

_____

_____

3. When we became criminals, alcoholics and/or drug addicts, crushed by a self-imposed crisis we could not postpone or evade; we had to fearlessly face the proposition that either God is everything or else He is nothing. God either is or He isn't. What is your choice to be?

_____

_____

_____

4. Can you come to the point of faith where you are willing to believe that a Living, Loving, Healing God can restore you to sanity?

_____

_____

_____

"I can do all things through Christ which strengthens me."
Philippians 4:13 (NKJV)

Step 3

"I now make a conscious decision to turn my will and my life over to the care of God."

"For whoever wants to save his own life will lose it: but whoever loses his life for My sake will find it."
Matthew 16:25 (HCSB)

Step 3 is an action step: Acknowledging that any life run on self-will is doomed to failure. If we are honest with ourselves we can look back in our lives and see what self-will has done to us. We have evidence that we are not in charge, although we continue to fight. I have a saying I use in the jails where I counsel:

"The more I try to control things outside of me the more self-control I lose."

We define this trait as self-centeredness, egocentricity, and playing with God. You have to decide to quit playing God and let God, our Heavenly Father, the Creator...be God. We solidify this decision with a prayer, called the *Third Step Prayer*, as used by Clarence S. and Dr. Bob.

Dear God,
I'm sorry about the mess I've made of my life.

I want to turn away from all the wrong things I've ever done and all the wrong things I've ever been. Please forgive me for it all.

I know You have the power to change my life and can turn me into a winner. Thank You, God for getting my attention long enough to interest me in trying it Your way.

God, please take over the management of my life and everything about me. I am making this conscious decision to turn my will and my life over to Your care and am asking You to please take over all parts of my life.

Please, God, move into my heart. However You do it is Your business, but makes Yourself real inside me and fill my awful emptiness. Fill me with your love and Holy Spirit and make me know Your will for me. And now, God, help Yourself to me and keep on doing it. I'm not sure I want You to, but do it anyhow.

I rejoice that I am now a part of Your people, that my uncertainty is gone forever, and that You now have control of my will and my life. Thank You and I praise Your name. Amen.

1. Have there been times when I have been unable to let go and trust God to care for the outcome of a particular situation? Describe.

   _____

   _____

   _____

2. What am I doing to reinforce my decision to allow my Higher Power to care for my will and my life?

   _____

   _____

   _____

3. Do I trust God enough to begin to let go? If not what is stopping me?

_____

_____

_____

4. Can my life improve without God? If so how?

_____

_____

_____

5. How does step 1 help with step 3?

_____

_____

_____

6. What action do I plan to take to follow through on my decision?

_____

_____

_____

Step 4

**"I agree to a searching and fearless
moral inventory of myself."**

The word searching means finding, so we are finding
ourselves. In doing so I must not be afraid. The pur-
pose of the first 3 steps was to get us to this point. We
cannot stop now. We have to write out what we did
wrong in order to get better; this is the moral part of
the step. Identifying our sins so we can see what we
have done, we can no longer hide from ourselves. We
must be completely honest in this step. This step will
cause anxiety; here are some tips to help.

*"Let no corrupt communication proceed out of your
mouth, but that which is good to the use of edifying,
that it may minister grace unto the hearers."*
Ephesians 4:29 (KJV)

*"And I saw the dead, small and great, stand before
God; and the books were opened: and another book
was opened, which is the book of life: and the dead
were judged out of those things which were written
in the books, according to their works."*
Revelation 20:12 (KJV)

1. What does the word moral mean to me?

_____

_____

_____

2. What are values?

_____

_____

_____

3. What are principles?

_____

_____

_____

We now have to embark on the journey back to the past and flush out the good and bad.

1. Do I have any resentment against my parents or caretakers? If so what are they and be detailed.

_____

_____

_____

2. Are there any institutions, schools, banks, Police Departments etc., that I hold resentments against? If so, what are they and be detailed.

_____

_____

_____

3. Did I act dishonestly in any of these situations? How?

_____

_____

_____

4. Did the resentments or dishonest acts affect my morals and spirit?

_____

_____

_____

5. Can I identify what I feel in uncomfortable situations? Identify the source of the discomfort.

_____

_____

_____

6. Have my feelings governed my actions? Give examples.

_____

_____

_____

7. What have I done to shut off or shut out my feelings?

_____

_____

_____

8. Are there feelings I am in denial about?

_____

_____

_____

9. What do I do when I try to deny my feelings?

_____

_____

_____

As we go through a short list of feelings, you will begin to feel a little uncomfortable. It is OK to feel today. You must not stop now, this is crucial. You have
to work through this portion and I recommend you go
through this part in one sitting. Some feelings we have
are imagined and this section helps decipher the difference between which are imagined and which are
real.

1. What is the difference between guilt and shame?

_____

_____

_____

2. What do I do when I feel guilt?

_____

_____

_____

3. What do I do when I feel shame?

_____

_____

_____

4. What do I feel guilty about? What part did I play in it, if any?

_____

_____

_____

5. What do I feel ashamed about? What part did I play in it, if any?

_____

_____

_____

Our relationships with others play a role in who we are; this area needs to be addressed.

1. What type of relationship did I have with my parents and/or caretakers? Be specific.

_____

_____

_____

2. What type of relationship did I have with my siblings? Be specific.

_____

_____

_____

3. Is it difficult for me to maintain healthy friendships? What in me makes it difficult?

_____

_____

_____

4. How do I fare in romantic relationships? Are they based solely on sex or are we truly compatible?

_____

_____

_____

5. Have I ever had a healthy romantic or friendship relationship? If so describe in detail why. If not, what character conflicts do I possess that prevent it?

_____

_____

_____

6. Has being hurt caused me to have trouble with intimacy?

_____

_____

_____

7. Do I damage platonic relationships for romantic ones?

_____

_____

_____

8. Do I have trouble keeping commitments?

_____

_____

_____

9. Has fear caused me to sacrifice and relationships? Explain.

_____

_____

_____

10. How has jail or other times I've been held against my will affected me? Describe in detail.

_____

_____

_____

11. Did I have a lot of friends in school? Why or why not?

_____

_____

_____

12. Can I have healthy relationships? What do I need to change in order to do so?

_____

_____

_____

Fear and worry comes from the belief that our problem is bigger that our God.

1. What are my fears?

_____

_____

_____

2. How have I let fear govern my life? Be specific.

_____

_____

_____

3. How do I cover my fears?

_____

_____

_____

4. Do my beliefs promote fear?

_____

_____

_____

5. Do I have faith in God?

_____

_____

_____

Sometimes we use sex to mask other feelings.

1. Do I use sex to cover up other feelings?

_____

_____

_____

2. Am I selfish regarding sex?

_____

_____

_____

3. Do I use sex to show love?

_____

_____

_____

4. Has sex left me feeling ashamed? If so describe.

_____

_____

_____

Most abusers have been abused.

1. Have I ever abused anyone? Describe

_____

_____

_____

2. Did I feel like a victim during my abusing, blaming others?

_____

_____

_____

3. Was I abused? If so by whom.

_____

_____

_____

4. Are there any other secrets I'm holding on to? If so what.

_____

_____

_____

We are not all bad. There are good things about us that our anti-social behavior has masked for years. It is time to look at the good in us too.

1. During my lifetime have I accomplished any goal I've set for myself? If so describe in detail.

_____

_____

_____

2. Have I ever promoted my values to others? If so what are they and when did I display them?

_____

_____

_____

3. What do I like about myself?

_____

_____

_____

4. What do I want to change?

_____

_____

_____

Step 5

"I admit to God, to myself, and to at least one other human-being, the exact nature of my wrongs."

"If we confess our sins, he is faithful and just to forgive us our sins, and to cleanse us from all unrighteousness."
1 John 1:9 (KJV)

"Therefore confess your sins to one another, and pray one for another, so that you may be healed. The prayer of the righteous is powerful and effective."
James 5:16 (NRSV)

This is not just a reading of the fourth step, it's a little deeper. It is now time to talk about why we did what we did, motives.

1. Can I talk about these crimes I committed against myself and others?

_____

_____

_____

2. Do I see the motives behind my anti-social behavior?

_____

_____

_____

3. Can I trust another human-being to share this with?

_____

_____

_____

4. Do I trust God for His forgiveness?

_____

_____

_____

Step 6

"I am entirely ready to have God remove all these defects of my character."

This step requires the willingness to change. We are not perfect and Rome wasn't built in a day. Up to this point we have put in a lot of work and should now have an intimate relationship with God. The key to living this step is to **TRUST GOD**.

"Indeed, we felt that we had received the sentence of death. But that was to make us rely not on ourselves but on God who raises the dead:
He delivered us from such a deadly peril,
and He will deliver us.
On Him we have set our hope that
He will deliver us again."
2 Corinthians 1:9, 10 (ESV)

It is suggested that you make a list of character defects you possess.

1. Is your list complete or did you hold back?

_____

_____

_____

2. Which defects do you want to keep? Why?

_____

_____

_____

3. Will getting rid of them hinder you? Explain.

_____

_____

_____

4. Do you really trust God?

_____

_____

_____

Step 7

**"I humbly ask God to remove my
defects and shortcomings."**

"Humility is our acceptance of ourselves, just the way
we are right now, understanding that we are not perfect, and doing all that we can do to improve ME."
(Author Unknown).

*"But now you must put them all away: anger, wrath,
malice, slander, blasphemy, and obscene talk.
Do not lie to one another, seeing that you have
put off the old self with its practices; and have put
on the new self, which is renewed in knowledge after
the image of its Creator."*
Colossians 3:8-10 (ESV)

By now we should be feeling better about ourselves.
We've put in a lot of work and might be tired. Don't
give up! It's a 12 step program.

Stopping now would rob you of the further benefits
the program has to offer. God helps those who help
themselves. This step has specific objectives.

1. Honesty and humility should become part of our character.

2. Continue growing in faith and seeking God's help.

3. Recognizing character old defects.

4. Trusting God to remove the defects and shortcomings.

5. Have a desire not to act out old behaviors.

6. Asking not to let you overlook any defects and shortcomings.

Here are a few questions we'll need to answer.

1. Are we ready?

_____
_____
_____

2. What effect will it have on me?

_____
_____
_____

3. What am I expecting to happen?

_____

_____

_____

4. How will this step change my life?

_____

_____

_____

5. What are you willing to do to help God remove the defects and promote the new behaviors?

_____

_____

_____

6. How will you and others notice the changes that have occurred?

_____

_____

_____

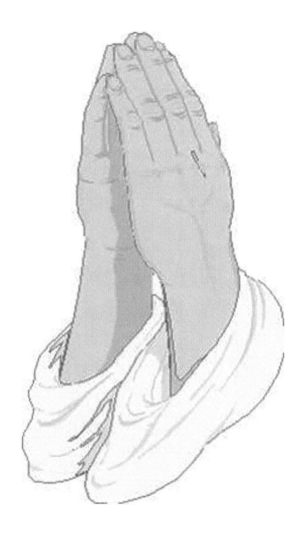

Step 8

"I agree to make a list of all persons I have harmed and am willing to make amends to them all."

Now it's time for restitution. Remember you are only making a list, don't jump ahead to actually making the amends yet. We have to practice faith in this step.

> *"For just as the body without the spirit is dead,*
> *So also faith without works is dead."*
> James 2:26 (NASB)

Begin our list starting with ourselves; we've done more damage to our selves than we ever imagined. We need to include everyone in our fourth step in this list.

1. Have you forgotten anyone? If so who?

_____

_____

_____

2. Are you afraid to put anyone on the list? If so who?

_____

_____

_____

3. Is there anyone you still hold resentment against?
   They should be on the list too.

_____

_____

_____

4. Will I trust God to guide me and not allow me to miss
   any one?

_____

_____

_____

Step 9

"I will make amends directly to such people wherever possible, except when to do so would injure them or others."

"Therefore if you bring your gift to the altar, and there remember that your brother has something against you, leave your gift there before the altar, and go your way. First be reconciled to your brother, and then come and offer your gift. Agree with your adversary quickly, while you are on the way with him; lest your adversary deliver you to the judge, the judge hand you over to the officer, and you be thrown into prison."
Matthew 5:23-25 (NKJV)

The restitution phase is only part done. Now that we've made a list, we have to put the amends into action.

1. Am I ready to make amends to these people?

_____

_____

_____

2. Have I asked God for guidance?

_____

_____

_____

3. Could I harm them by contacting them?

_____

_____

_____

4. Could I honestly harm myself in any way by contacting them?

_____

_____

_____

5. How will I contact them? In person, phone, letter, etc.?

_____

_____

_____

6. What action plan will follow?

_____

_____

_____

7. What if they don't accept my amends?

_____

_____

_____

8. How will I respond to criticism and rejection?

_____

_____

_____

Once this is done we will feel a sense of freedom. The past can no longer haunt us. We have forgiven ourselves and sought forgiveness from those we have harmed. If we can't make amends to a person, for whatever reason, we ask for God's forgiveness and not do it again. We are now ready to move into the maintenance phase.

"Blessed is he whose transgressions *are forgiven,* whose sins are covered.

Blessed is the man whose sin the Lord does not count against him and in whose spirit is no deceit."

Psalms 32:1-2

(NIV)

Step 10

"I will continue to take personal inventory and when I am wrong I will promptly admit it."

*"Reckless words pierce like a sword,
but the tongue of the wise brings healing.
Truthful lips endure forever
but a lying tongue lasts only a moment.
There is deceit in the hearts of those who plot evil
but joy for those who promote peace."*
Proverbs 12:18-20 (NIV)

We have to give ourselves a "check-up" from the neck up daily. If we relax we will fall into the same habits with the same people.

1. What are my thoughts on?

_____

_____

_____

2. What are my feelings?

_____

_____

_____

3. What is the risk factor I'm facing right now?

_____

_____

_____

4. Have I caused any conflicts today?

_____

_____

_____

5. Will I have to add another person on my next eighth step?

_____

_____

_____

6. What have I done to stay in God's favor?

_____

_____

_____

7. Do I volunteer to help anywhere outside of my home or a meeting?

_____

_____

_____

Keeping track of our daily thoughts and activities helps provide a safeguard against negative, anti-social behavior.

Step 11

**"I seek, through prayer and meditation, to improve
my conscious contact with God, praying only
for the knowledge of God's will for me and the
power to carry that out."**

*"Blessed are the poor in spirit: for theirs is the kingdom
of heaven. Blessed are those who hunger and thirst
for righteousness: for they will be filled.*
Matthew 5:3, 6 (NIV)

Our second and third steps are reinforced in this step.
I now have to surrender and turn it over on a deeper
level.

1. How does your commitment to Ex-Offenders Anonymous increase your commitment to God?

_____

_____

_____

2. How often do I pray?

_____

_____

_____

3. Is there a certain time or situation happening when I pray?

_____

_____

_____

4. How often do I meditate?

_____

_____

_____

5. Do I have a specific time to meditate?

_____

_____

_____

6. What is the difference between God's will and self-will

_____

_____

_____

7. Have I found out God's will for me or do I still operate in self-will?

_____

_____

_____

8. Have I ever sacrificed my beliefs for personal gain?

_____

_____

_____

Upon completion of this step I should be able to understand and carry- out God's will for my life.

Step 12

"I, having had a spiritual awakening and as a result of an effort to practice these principles in my daily life, will carry this message to other ex offenders who have a desire to change."

"Whosoever will come after me, let him deny himself, and take up his cross, and follow me. For whosoever will save his life shall lose it; but whosoever shall lose his life for my sake and the gospel's, the same shall save it. Or what shall a man give in exchange for his soul?
St. Mark 8:34-35, 37 (KJV)

1. Have I had a spiritual awakening?

_____

_____

_____

2. What am I willing to give away in order to keep what I have?

_____

_____

_____

3. Have I changed as a result of this program?

_____

_____

_____

4. How will I carry the message?

_____

_____

_____

5. How will I show gratitude to God and this program?

_____

_____

_____

Here are a few suggestions on carrying the message.

1. Walk the talk.

2. Stay in contact with other members of the program.

3. Share your recovery with others who <u>want</u> help.

4. Visit others who need help.

5. Sponsor another member.

6. Volunteer your time in and out of the program.

7. Speak so others can here the message.

8. Become a guide for others through their struggle.

We must formulate a personal Relapse Prevention Plan (RPP) to identify risk factors and triggers we have. It also helps us to plan what to do when the factors/triggers arise. This plan can be modified as new risk factors/triggers are found. We now have insight on what makes us tick.

Congratulations
on making it through
all 12 Steps!

Now that you have completed the **12 Steps** it's time to start over from step one. As life changes so do we and we want ensure our changes stay positive so we start over to stay healthy. The only thing constant in life is change.

ACKNOWLEDGEMENTS

I'd like to thank the following: F.I.S.T. Inc and Joe Schmitt for having faith in me to take on this venture. My children for making me want to be a better man and father. I would also like to thank AA, for starting the 12 step concept and NA for taking the 12 step concept to a different level. NICASA organization for helping me when I needed it most and giving me the opportunity to give back in a way I never dreamed imaginable, through that opportunity I was introduced to Joe Schmitt, founder of F.I.S.T. Inc

There are many more who contributed in one way or another and I'd like to thank them too.

We began this venture with reviewing the works of Dr.Francis Deisler and Dr. Kevin Stewart who developed the original workbook *U.S. Offenders Anonymous* for therapist to work with clients. It is my hope that this work book can be used for ex-offenders to work with ex-offenders and their mentors, on a road to be better citizens.

Most of all I'd like to thank God; we are strong believers in Christ and believe that without Him, nothing is possible. If this workbook can help just one person, then it was not in vain.

Made in the USA
Columbia, SC
09 January 2020

86390633R00038